To everyone who has fallen off. J.M.

To my mom, dad, Tiz, and Lule: thanks for everything. E.

First published in Great Britain 2023 by Red Shed, part of Farshore
An imprint of HarperCollins*Publishers*
1 London Bridge Street, London SE1 9GF
www.farshore.co.uk

HarperCollins*Publishers*
Macken House, 39/40 Mayor Street Upper, Dublin 1, D01 C9W8

Text copyright © James May 2023
James May has asserted his moral rights.
Illustrations copyright © HarperCollins*Publishers* 2023
Illustrated by Emans.
Photograph of James May by Ellis O'Brien.

ISBN 978 0 00 852087 8
Printed and bound in Italy.
001

A CIP catalogue record for this title is available from the British Library.

Stay safe online. Any website addresses listed in this book are correct at the time of going to print.
However, Farshore is not responsible for content hosted by third parties. Please be aware that online
content can be subject to change and websites can contain content that is unsuitable for children.
We advise that all children are supervised when using the internet.

Farshore takes its responsibility to the planet and its inhabitants very seriously.
We aim to use papers from well-managed forests run by responsible suppliers.

JAMES MAY

MARVELLOUS VEHICLES

ILLUSTRATED BY

EMANS

RED SHED

INTRODUCTION

This book is all about very special vehicles; there are no engines or electric motors driving any of them . . . because they are all human powered.

But what counts as a human-powered vehicle? Well, it is any means of transport that doesn't involve another source of power (such as an engine or an animal) and doesn't require fuel (other than your food, but you were going to eat that anyway). So no electric scooters, because that's cheating, and no sand yachts, because they use the wind.

I'm fascinated by human-powered vehicles. I've been lucky in my life to have driven the world's greatest cars. I've also driven lorries and buses, flown light aircraft and sailed motor boats. But the mode of transport I use the most – almost every day – is my bicycle.

There's something very satisfying about bowling along using nothing more than your own muscles for power. And despite all of the technology we've invented, human-powered vehicles still make sense: they are good for you because they're a form of exercise; they don't produce pollution; and they are free to use, which isn't true of anything needing petrol or electricity.
What marvellous vehicles.

My first vehicle was a human-powered vehicle – of course it was, as I was only three years old. It was a simple scoot-along trike. Then I had a pedal car (my first car, and possibly the one I loved the most) and eventually I discovered bicycles. The bicycle gave me my first taste of true freedom. I took it apart, modified it and repainted it. I still do this with bicycles today and have a collection of them.

There's more to the world of human-powered vehicles than bicycles, though. You might be surprised by how many ways there are of moving around using nothing more than the power of our own bodies. Some are a bit silly, like the pogo stick, but many are important to the way the world works: skis and rowing boats, for example.

It's likely that the first vehicle ever made by people was a human-powered vehicle – a log canoe. We've been powering ourselves ever since. I hope you enjoy reading about these remarkable machines and maybe even have a go on a few yourselves.

So, are you ready to join me and find out more about them? Jump on your bike or scooter, get in your velomobile or submarine (yes, really!), and off we go.

James May

POWERED BY YOU

Human-powered vehicles are all about 'energy management'.
Whatever your human-powered vehicle, energy takes
two forms – potential energy and kinetic energy.
Here's what that means . . .

Potential energy

1. The potential energy of a human-powered vehicle is the energy it has because it is raised above the ground. On your scooter at the top of a ramp, you have potential energy, because gravity will pull you and your scooter down the slope of the ramp and speed you up.

2. Kinetic energy is the energy a thing has because it is moving. Riding along on your scooter, you have kinetic energy. This can power you at least some of the way up the next ramp. You are using the energy you gained coming down the previous hill.

Kinetic energy

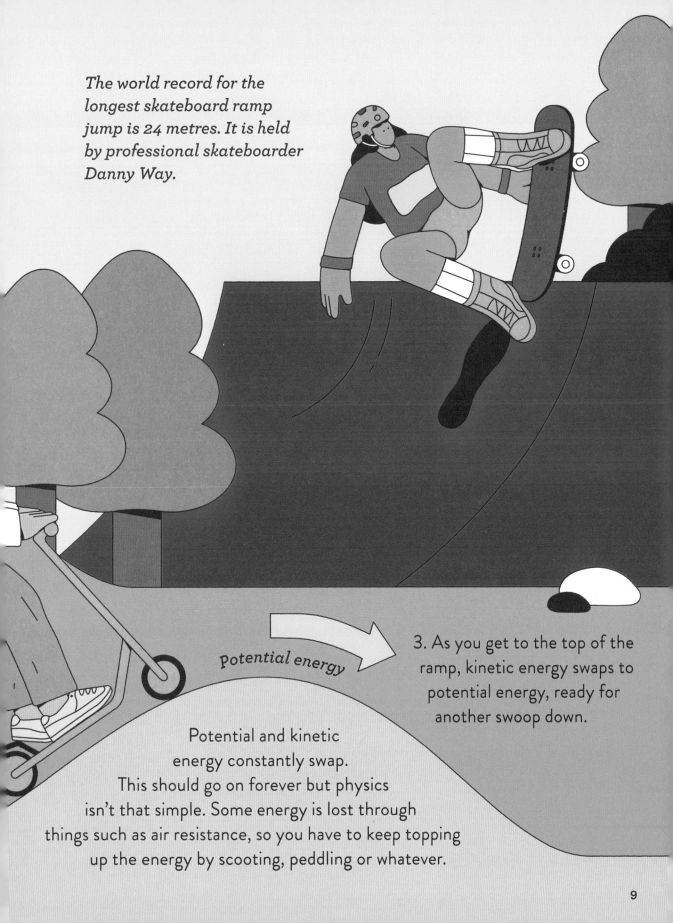

The world record for the longest skateboard ramp jump is 24 metres. It is held by professional skateboarder Danny Way.

potential energy

3. As you get to the top of the ramp, kinetic energy swaps to potential energy, ready for another swoop down.

Potential and kinetic energy constantly swap. This should go on forever but physics isn't that simple. Some energy is lost through things such as air resistance, so you have to keep topping up the energy by scooting, peddling or whatever.

THE NEED FOR SPEED

Human-powered vehicles are all about moving along more quickly and efficiently than by walking or running. The world's fastest runner can reach over 40 kilometres per hour. Want to beat that? Try these . . .

Roller skates and blades speed up walking – they make each step bigger and you can freewheel. Less exhausting and quicker than walking, but not good for stairs.

Roller skates were invented in the 1760s.

Skateboarding is now an Olympic sport. Once a skateboard is scooted up to speed incredible stunts can be performed.

The basic wheelchair is powered by arms. Specialised, lightweight chairs are built for racing and sports, such as wheelchair basketball.

The wheelchair is one of the few vehicles that can turn around in its own length.

Skis are fast downhill and even work on level ground with the help of ski poles. They are vital for polar exploration as it's difficult to walk on soft snow.

I had a toboggan crash aged 16. I went down a long hill and hit the fence at the bottom.

Toboggans look like a free ride, with no effort needed. But that's not true, because they only work downhill – you have to pull them up a hill first. You can't use a chairlift because that's cheating.

Ice skates are designed to allow you to move quickly across ice. The blade shape means they slide forwards and backwards but grip side-to-side, which allows for steering.

Ice skates have little friction, so speed skaters can go as fast as cars.

BRILLIANT BICYCLES

My favourite. And the most energy-efficient form of transport ever. You can go up to five times as far on a bike as you can on foot for the same effort. The lumpy act of walking turns into smooth circular motion.

Most bikes have a frame and two wheels of equal size. When you push down on the foot pedals, power is transferred to the rear wheel through a chain or belt. There is huge variety in design . . .

Folding bikes have become popular in cities because they're easy to store and can be taken on other transport, such as trains and buses.

A unicycle is less than half a bike, and the pedals are attached directly to the wheel. There are also no brakes. I tried a unicycle once but faceplanted.

Some people prefer to lie back on a bike.
Recumbent bikes are kind to your joints
and muscles, and are very stable.

*A flag helps other road users
see a recumbent bike.*

*The very first bikes
were made from wood.*

Mountain bikes are
for riding off-road.
They have fat tyres
and lots of gears to
make pedalling easier
on rough surfaces.

Racers and road bikes are built
for speed: they are lightweight
and have thin tyres.

The pedals on a handcycle are in
front of you and turned with your
hands. A handcycle is used for
fitness training and by people
with leg injuries or limb differences.

13

HUMAN-POWERED CARS

Not old enough to drive yet? Don't worry – I was already driving by the age of five. I had an E-Type Jag but I had to use my legs to make it go.

I LOVE cars. Maybe it's because I loved my E-Type Jag so much. It was dark blue with a white steering wheel and polished spoked wheels.

Pedal cars for very young drivers have to be small, which is a challenge for designers as there isn't enough space for bicycle pedals. The solution is . . .

Pedal car

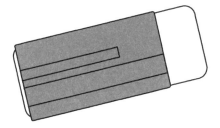

. . . to have a pair of treadles instead of pedals. These are linked by rods to cranks on the rear axle. You have to push each treadle at exactly the right moment, when the crank is at the top of its rotation, otherwise you won't move. It's a tricky technique and I was never very good at it.

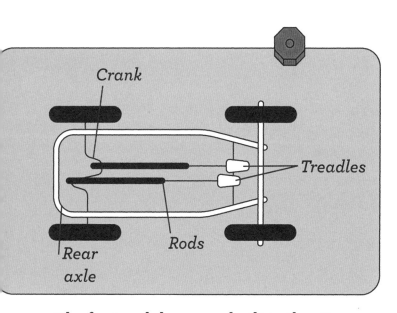

Crank

Treadles

Rods

Rear axle

The first pedal car was built in the 1890s, not long after the first engine-powered car.

Pedal go-karts and bigger pedal cars are easier to drive because they're driven by pedals and a chain, like a bicycle. My brother had a pedal go-kart similar to the one in the drawing below, but he wouldn't let me drive it.

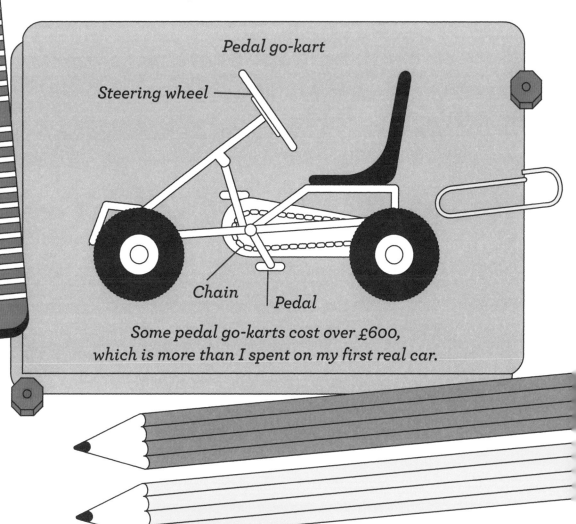

Pedal go-kart

Steering wheel

Chain

Pedal

Some pedal go-karts cost over £600, which is more than I spent on my first real car.

Try designing your own human-powered car. There's a lot to think about: pedals or treadles? Thin tyres for speed or fat tyres for grip? Remember it can't be too heavy or it will be tiring to ride. So have a think about materials – would you choose plastic, metal, wood or something else? Would you add gears? What about brakes?

But what about a vehicle that has the energy efficiency of a bike AND the weather protection and practicality of a car? Meet the velomobile. Here is a cutaway of one so you can see the pedals and chain inside.

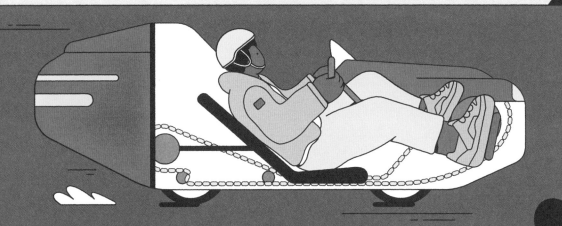

What about arm-powered cars? Yes, we've invented those too. The mechanism we saw in a small pedal car (using a crank to drive the wheels), is also in a handcar (or draisine).

People use their arms to pump a beam up and down – a bit like a see-saw – to drive the crank mechanism.

Like a small pedal car, you have to push at the right moment, or you stop the wheels instead of turning them.

There's even space in the back of a velomobile to put your belongings.

Handcars were used in the past by railway workers to travel short distances and check the track for damage. They had to be light so humans could produce enough power to move them. And also because users had to be able to lift the car off the track if a real train came along. Now that's what I call . . . handy!

THE WONDER OF WATER

Let's move from pedals to paddles and look at some of the earliest human-powered vehicles: boats. Humans used them to cross rivers and seas, long before they figured out how to make bridges.

Early boats were simple. The most basic was a log – people balanced on it and used their hands as paddles.

Then, around 10,000 years ago, somebody worked out that if you hollow out a log, you can sit *in* it. This makes it more stable. All rowed and paddled boats are a version of this idea.

The first kayaks were made from animal skin and bone.

The great thing about travelling by boat is there are no hills on water, and at low speed the water gives little resistance. So one good heave on the oars or paddle of a boat will send you quite a long way.

But how about adding some mechanisms? Most human-powered hydrofoils (below left) are driven by pedals and a propeller. They have underwater wings that lift up the craft as it moves through the water.

Even more fun is the Aquaskipper (below right), invented by Shane Chen. You jump up and down on a giant spring, which pushes a paddle to send you forwards – like a pogo stick for water.

If you stop pedalling a hydrofoil or jumping on an Aquaskipper, you sink!

Pedaloes have a pedal mechanism that turns either a boat propeller or a paddle wheel. Pedaloes come in all sorts of designs.

Pedaloes can be shaped like swans, but I've driven one shaped like a giant banana.

SUPER SUBMARINES

Believe it or not, the first working submarine was human-powered. That's because it was built in 1620, when the only means of powering boats were sails or oars. As sails won't work underwater, it had to have oars.

This 'diving boat' (the word 'submarine' hadn't been invented yet) was built from a wooden frame covered with waterproofed leather. It travelled about four metres below the River Thames, in London.

It's difficult to see a practical use for human-powered submarines today, but they are still built by engineering students who race them around underwater courses.

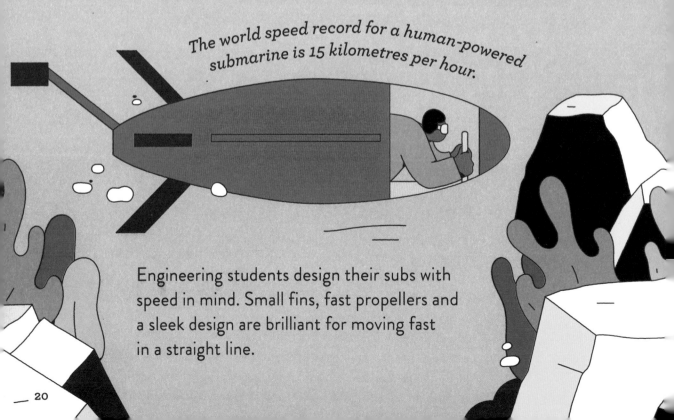

The world speed record for a human-powered submarine is 15 kilometres per hour.

Engineering students design their subs with speed in mind. Small fins, fast propellers and a sleek design are brilliant for moving fast in a straight line.

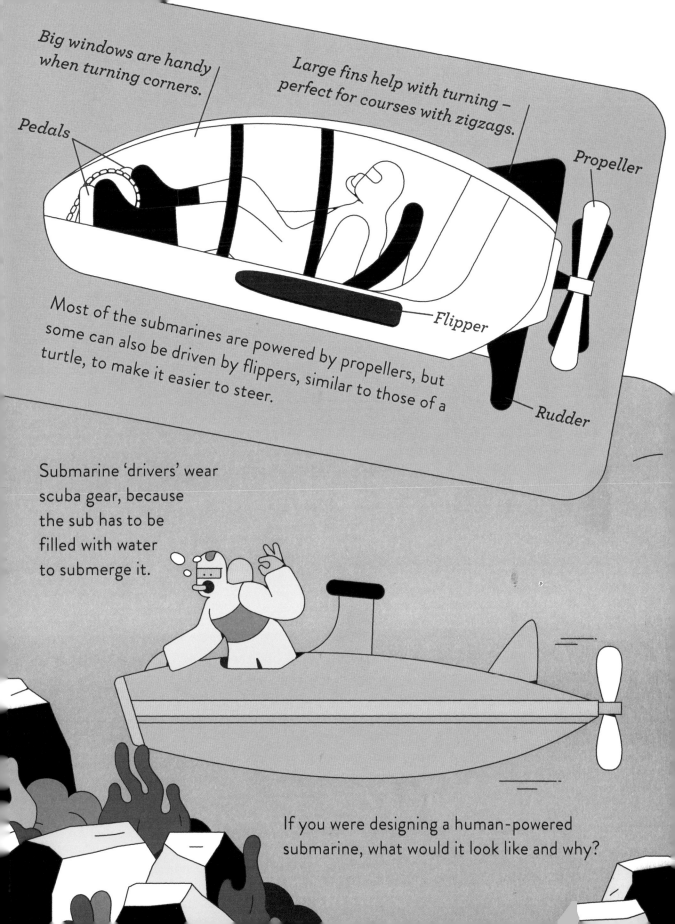

Big windows are handy when turning corners.

Large fins help with turning – perfect for courses with zigzags.

Pedals

Propeller

Flipper

Most of the submarines are powered by propellers, but some can also be driven by flippers, similar to those of a turtle, to make it easier to steer.

Rudder

Submarine 'drivers' wear scuba gear, because the sub has to be filled with water to submerge it.

If you were designing a human-powered submarine, what would it look like and why?

AMPHIBIOUS ANTICS

Amphibious cars are ones that can be driven on the road AND in the water. They have never been very successful and have a history of sinking. Can human-powered amphibious vehicles do better?

I love bicycles and the earliest amphibious bicycle is the Cyclomer, built in 1932. But it didn't work at all. The wheels were designed to float, and they did, but they wouldn't grip the road OR power the bike on the water. So it wasn't much use.

Float

Hollow wheel

Autocanoes are for bicycle and canoe fans. In water the two front wheels become paddles, and the rear wheel becomes a rudder for steering.

Mohammad Saidullah's invention is a normal bike fitted with fold-down, air-filled 'pontoons' (like miniature boats) to keep it afloat. You pedal it through the water. And guess what? This one actually works.

Pontoon

The Shuttle Bike Kit, designed by Roberto Siviero, includes inflatable pontoons and a shaft that runs from the bike mechanisms to drive a proper propeller.

All parts are carried in a rucksack. When you get to water, it takes about 15 minutes to assemble.

Shaft

Pontoon

UP IN THE AIR

We've seen how human power can help us travel across land and water. And, unbelievably, it can take us through the sky too.

The most basic human-powered aircraft is the hang-glider. It is launched from a hill or a cliff, so first you have to climb up there. Your human power is used in gaining potential energy.

Take a run-up and launch into the air to convert potential energy into kinetic energy. Pilots can find winds to climb higher, but really a hang-glider is just making a long landing.

I've flown some amazing planes since getting my pilot's licence, but none of them have been quite like the human-powered Gossamer Albatross. It is driven by pedals and a chain – so the pilot needs to be a very fit cyclist. If they stop pedalling, it will crash!

The Albatross, designed by Paul MacCready, flew from England to France in 1979 at a top speed of 29 kilometres per hour at a height of just 1.5 metres.

Minus the pilot, it weighs just 32 kilograms – about the same as a large dog.

— Propeller

Pedals —

In the 15th century, Leonardo da Vinci sketched an 'aerial screw'. It was a bit like a human-powered helicopter, but would have been too heavy to actually fly.

Engineers cracked it in 2013, and the human-powered helicopter became real. Aerovelo's pedal-powered Atlas hovered for one minute – a world first.

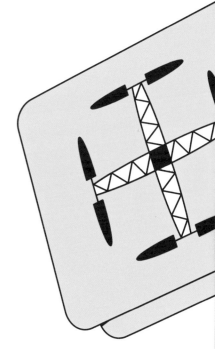

HOW FAR CAN WE GO?

I hope you've enjoyed this quick gallop through human-powered vehicles. The variety is amazing, isn't it? I think we can divide them into three categories.

Some human-powered vehicles are for fun and sport: hang-gliders, skates and skateboards are used for competitions. Things like pogo sticks and the Aquaskipper are really just a bit of a laugh.

Some are useful, most noticeably the bicycle. As cities become more congested and people worry about pollution and health, a bicycle answers a lot of problems. A groceries delivery company near me has ditched vans and now only uses bikes.

Skis, rowing boats, and wheelchairs also come under 'useful'. I don't ski, though, because I hate snow.

Then there are exotic human-powered vehicles – aeroplanes, helicopters and submarines. These aren't 'useful'. Instead, they are engineering exercises because building them involves great challenges.

A human develops only up to one half of one horsepower (hp). A small car engine produces around 75hp. So if you're designing a helicopter to be powered by one human, you have to think carefully about things such as weight, friction and air resistance. Engineers enjoy this stuff, and it helps develop their thinking on things such as new materials.

WHAT'S NEXT?

Developments in battery technology mean that we can now have human power with a bit of help. Think of the electric-assist bicycle – you still have to pedal but its small electric motor makes it easier. I think we'll see more of this hybrid of human power with electrical assistance in the future with vehicles such as pedaloes and go-karts. It's clean and quiet, and you still do a bit of exercise.

Just how far can human power take us? Who knows? But I do know that this story is far from over. For now, though, I'm off out on my bike.

GLOSSARY

air resistance – A type of friction between air and an object, which hinders it moving through the air.

axle – The spinning shaft on which a wheel or gear turns.

crank – A bent portion of a shaft that allows you to turn back-and-forth motion into circular motion.

friction – A force that resists one object sliding against another.

gears – Wheels with teeth that can be used to change the speed. In bicycles, for example, they make pedalling easier or harder.

horsepower – A figure indicating the 'strength' of a machine, originally used to compare steam engines with the horses they replaced.

kinetic energy – The energy a thing has because it is moving.

paddle wheel – A semi-submerged wheel, with blades running cross-wise, that rotates, so it pushes a craft through water.

physics – The science of matter and energy. A big subject that includes the forces at work in human-powered vehicles.

potential energy – For a human-powered vehicle, this is the energy it has because it is raised above the ground.

---

recumbent – A fancy way of saying 'lying down on your back'.

---

rods – Rigid connections between moving parts.

---

treadles – A type of pedal that goes back and forth instead of round and round.

About the Author
James May is a writer and broadcaster. He is best known for co-presenting *The Grand Tour* and *Top Gear*, and his previous books for adults include *Carbolics* and *Car Fever*. This is James's first book officially for children.

About the Illustrator
Emans is an Italian-Brazilian illustrator who currently lives and works in Italy. He has always been passionate about visual arts, and studied graphics in Buenos Aires, Argentina.